UNSCARRED
MY FREEDOM STORY

HEATHER SCHOTT

Unscarred: My Freedom Story

Copyright 2023 by Heather Schott

ISBN: 979-8-9881690-5-5

All rights reserved. No part of *Unscarred: My Freedom Story* may be reproduced, stored in a retrieval system, or transmitted in any form or by any means—by electronic, mechanical, photocopying, recording or otherwise—without permission. Thank you for buying an authorized edition of this book and for complying with copyright laws.

Unless otherwise noted, Scripture quotations are taken from The ESV® Bible (The Holy Bible, English Standard Version®), copyright © 2001 by Crossway, a publishing ministry of Good News Publishers. Used by permission. All rights reserved.

Scripture quotations marked AMPC are from the Amplified® Bible (AMPC), Copyright © 1954, 1958, 1962, 1964, 1965, 1987 by The Lockman Foundation. Used by permission. www.Lockman.org

Scripture quotations marked BSB are from The Holy Bible, Berean Study Bible, copyright © 2016 by Bible Hub. Used by permission. All rights reserved worldwide.

Scripture quotations marked CSB have been taken from the Christian Standard Bible®, Copyright © 2017 by Holman Bible Publishers. Used by permission. Christian Standard Bible® and CSB® are federally registered trademarks of Holman Bible Publishers.

Scripture quotations marked NASB are taken from the (NASB®) New American Standard Bible®, Copyright © 1960, 1971, 1977, 1995, 2020 by The Lockman Foundation. Used by permission. All rights reserved. www.lockman.org

Scripture quotations marked NIRV are taken from the Holy Bible, New International Reader's Version®, NIrV® Copyright © 1995, 1996, 1998, 2014 by Biblica, Inc.® Used by permission of Zondervan. All rights reserved worldwide. www.zondervan.com. The "NIrV" and "New International Reader's Version" are trademarks registered in the United States Patent and Trademark Office by Biblica, Inc.®

Scripture quotations marked NIV are taken from the Holy Bible, New International Version®, NIV®. Copyright © 1973, 1978, 1984, 2011 by Biblica, Inc.™ Used by permission of Zondervan. All rights reserved worldwide. www.zondervan.com. The "NIV" and "New International Version" are trademarks registered in the United States Patent and Trademark Office by Biblica, Inc.™

Scripture quotations marked NKJV are taken from the New King James Version®. Copyright © 1982 by Thomas Nelson. Used by permission. All rights reserved.

Scripture quotations marked NLT are taken from the Holy Bible, New Living Translation, copyright ©1996, 2004, 2015 by Tyndale House Foundation. Used by permission of Tyndale House Publishers, Carol Stream, Illinois 60188. All rights reserved.

Printed in the United States

Dear Writer,

Now is the time to write your freedom story! Why? Because Revelation 12:10–11 says, "And I heard a loud voice in heaven, saying, 'Now the salvation and the power and the kingdom of our God and the authority of his Christ have come, for the accuser of our brothers has been thrown down, who accuses them day and night before our God. And they have conquered him by the blood of the Lamb and by the word of their testimony, for they loved not their lives even unto death.'" The Bible says you conquer the devil by the blood of the Lamb and the word of your testimony—your testimony is your freedom story, what Christ has done for you!

But how about also asking yourself, "Why not?" The why nots usually have to do with fear of hurting someone else, fear of digging up the past, fear of facing what you did, fear of what people will think…Do you see the common thread here? Fear. Fear keeps us bound; it keeps us living a life we don't want; fear keeps us paralyzed. You will never like the outcome of a fear-based decision. It may seem like the easy route in the moment, but facing what you need to face with the Lord (no matter how ugly it is) will always have a better outcome than partnering with fear.

The other reason many don't write out their story is that of the excuse "I don't have the time." We under-spiritualize some of the most important and easiest tools for freedom God has given us. Can you imagine if Paul would have decided he didn't have the time in his busy schedule of traveling; being persecuted, imprisoned, and in shipwrecks; and more to write down his story and experiences? Can you imagine where we would be without the books of Romans, Galatians, and 1 and 2 Corinthians, and many other books in the New Testament written by Paul? This is why it's time to write your freedom story. It's a giant step toward freedom and not just freedom for you but freedom for others.

I remember struggling to write my story in the beginning. In fact, I had so many thoughts of fear and felt so much anxiety I put it off for years despite prophetic word after prophetic word saying, "It's time to write your story." The encouraging part but also the nerve-racking part of the prophetic words also said this: "Your story is going to bring so much healing and freedom for others." So, I pass this on to you today: your story will not just be a huge step of freedom for you but will heal and set so many others free. This is why you feel the nerves you do, or overwhelmed or fear or whatever that nagging thought or feeling is. This is why you will feel the resistance to writing and sharing—whether you do now or not, I'm sure in some part of this process you will feel resistance. Let me encourage you, bring courage to you—this means you are on the right track! You are pleasing the Lord, you are fighting for freedom, and this is beautiful! This is worth fighting for! The Lord also believes it's worth fighting for, and He will fight for you! So lean in to Him; encounter Him as you write; turn on worship music as you write. Pause to pray and ask Him to remind you of moments, and let Him heal you and then guide you as you write those moments! Joshua 1:9 says, "Have I not commanded you? Be strong and courageous. Do not be frightened, and do not be dismayed, for the L ORD *your God is with you wherever you go." Be courageous! And then rest in Him, knowing He is with you!*

So writer, take a deep breath in and invite the Holy Spirit into the room you're in right now. Invite Him to speak to you. Invite Him into this beautiful process of writing your freedom story so that others may be set free also!

With love,

Now it's time to write your freedom story...

"For the accuser of our brothers has been thrown down—he who accuses them day and night before our God. They have conquered him by the blood of the Lamb and by the word of their testimony."
—Revelation 12:10–11, BSB

"Be free! Share your testimony! And conquer the accuser!"

"Therefore, if anyone is in Christ, he is a new creation. The old has passed away; behold, the new has come."
—2 Corinthians 5:17

> *"Share your testimony! Write it all down! Then shout it from the rooftops! Roar and let everyone around you hear what God has done in your life!"*
>
> —HB

"So if the Son sets you free, you will be free indeed."
—John 8:36

"Satan no longer has authority over you. You are no longer in bondage—you are no longer in his prison of shame, but you are set free, as is your voice!"

> "The righteous thrive like a palm tree and grow like a cedar tree in Lebanon. Planted in the house of the Lord, they thrive in the courts of our God. They will still bear fruit in old age, healthy and green, to declare, 'The Lord is just; he is my rock, and there is no unrighteousness in him.'"
> —Psalm 92:12–15, csb

"God, I desire the unscarred life, where You promise to take the old and give me new life."

—KB

> "As far as the east is from the west, so far has he removed our transgressions from us."
> —Psalm 103:12, CSB

"The greater the influence on your life, the greater the war over the influence you carry."

—HB

"If your life and dreams are really His, it doesn't matter what you look like or what accusations come against you when you're obeying the Lord!"

—HB

> "'No weapon that is formed against you will succeed; and you will condemn every tongue that accuses you in judgment. This is the heritage of the servants of the Lord, and their vindication is from Me,' declares the Lord."
> —Isaiah 54:17, NASB

*"My soul, bless the L*ORD*, and do not forget all his benefits. He forgives all your iniquity; he heals all your diseases. He redeems your life from the Pit; he crowns you with faithful love and compassion."*
—PSALM 103:2–4, CSB

> "We give thanks to you, O God; we give thanks, for your name is near. We recount your wondrous deeds."
> —Psalm 75:1

> *"Remember, God is the One who is fighting for you. He loves you like no person is capable of doing."*
> —KB

*"I have been young, and now am old, yet I have
not seen the righteous forsaken."*
—Psalm 37:25

"For the Lord loves justice and will not abandon his faithful ones. They are kept safe forever."
—Psalm 37:28, csb

"God has chosen you from the beginning to be saved by the sanctification of the Spirit and by faith in the truth."
—2 Thessalonians 2:13, BSB

"When you refuse to hide your past, it cannot control you anymore."
—HB

> "The thief comes only to steal and kill and destroy. I came that they may have life and have it abundantly."
> —John 10:10

> *"You don't have to live a perfect life—you just have to live for the perfect One, Jesus. He will use your imperfections to glorify Himself and set others free."*
>
> —HB

"And he who was seated on the throne said, 'Behold, I am making all things new.' Also he said, 'Write this down, for these words are trustworthy and true.'"

—Revelation 21:5

"Evidence of a life change is hardly recognizing the new you and hardly identifying with the old you."

—HB

> "For freedom Christ has set us free; stand firm therefore,
> and do not submit again to a yoke of slavery."
> —Galatians 5:1

> *"Live as people who are free, not using your freedom as a cover-up for evil, but living as servants of God."*
> —1 PETER 2:16

"Listen to conviction, not worry or fear."

> *"I sought the LORD, and he answered me and rescued me from all my fears."*
> —PSALM 34:4, CSB

> "Come and hear, all you who fear God, and I
> will tell what he has done for my soul."
> —Psalm 66:16

"Conviction is a beautiful thing; it is your best form of accountability—it is with you when others are not."

—HS

> "When the Spirit of truth comes, he will guide you into all truth. He will not speak on his own but will tell you what he has heard."
> —John 16:13, NLT

> "The Lord challenges us with His truth not to condemn us but to convict us to bring us into right standing with Him so we can move forward in unity with Him!"
>
> —HB

> "So Jesus said to the Jews who had believed him, 'If you abide in my word, you are truly my disciples, and you will know the truth, and the truth will set you free.'"
> —JOHN 8:31–32

*"Now the Lord is the Spirit, and where the
Spirit of the Lord is, there is freedom."*
—2 Corinthians 3:17

"Jesus does not condemn; He brings conviction, to bring repentance, to bring freedom!"

—HB

"For God did not send his Son into the world to condemn the world, but in order that the world might be saved through him."
—John 3:17

> "The Lord is my strength and my song, and he has become my salvation; this is my God, and I will praise him, my father's God, and I will exalt him."
> —Exodus 15:2

> *"He is so rich in kindness and grace that he purchased our freedom with the blood of his Son and forgave our sins."*
> —Ephesians 1:7, NLT

"Forgiveness will bring you freedom, and freedom will bring you so much healing!"

—HB

"For you, Lord, are kind and ready to forgive, abounding in faithful love to all who call on you."
—Psalm 86:5, CSB

"...bearing with one another and, if one has a complaint against another, forgiving each other; as the Lord has forgiven you, so you also must forgive."
—Colossians 3:13

> *"Look beyond the circumstances you are in right now and learn to let go and forgive!"*
> —HB

*"But if you do not forgive others their sins, your
Father will not forgive your sins."*
—Matthew 6:15, niv

> *"Humility takes intentionality; it takes passion; it takes an all-in heart that is sold-out for true freedom!"*
>
> —HB

"Humble yourselves before the Lord, and he will exalt you."
—James 4:10

"He leads the humble in what is right, and teaches the humble his way."
—Psalm 25:9

"*Humility is about* submitting *to the* process *(no one is fixed overnight) and allowing accountability.*"

—HB

> *"For the Lord takes pleasure in his people; he adorns the humble with salvation."*
> —Psalm 149:4

"I promise you this: the fruit of humility is worth every humbling moment!"

—HB

"But he gives more grace. Therefore it says, 'God opposes the proud but gives grace to the humble.'"
—James 4:6

"Humility is about lowering yourself and getting rid of pride and that puffed-up defensive thing that rises up in us."

—HB

> *"Humility is the fear of the Lord; its wages are riches and honor and life."*
> —Proverbs 22:4, NIV

"This level of humility brings healing."

—HB

> *"The LORD is near the brokenhearted; he saves those crushed in spirit."*
> —PSALM 34:18, CSB

> "Do not fear, for I have redeemed you; I have called you by name; you are Mine."
> —Isaiah 43:1, NASB

"You are called to live out your purpose, not someone else's."
—HB

"Let the redeemed of the Lord say so, whom he has redeemed from trouble."
—Psalm 107:2

"You were designed to do what only you can do, while others were designed to do what only they can do."

—HB

"A person's steps are established by the Lord, and he takes pleasure in his way. Though he falls, he will not be overwhelmed, because the Lord supports him with his hand."
—Psalm 37:23–24, csb

"He brought me up from a desolate pit, out of the muddy clay, and set my feet on a rock, making my steps secure."
—Psalm 40:2, CSB

"Stop comparing yourself with others and what they had that you didn't. That comparison will keep you in bondage."

*"Those who look to him are radiant with joy;
their faces will never be ashamed."*
—Psalm 34:5, CSB

"*I am at rest in God alone; my salvation comes from him. He alone is my rock and my salvation, my stronghold; I will never be shaken.*"
—Psalm 62:1–2, CSB

> *"When we accept Christ as our Savior, we are confronting and repenting for the crooked ways in our lives and saying yes to the straight and narrow path that leads to eternal life with Jesus!"*
>
> —HK

*"God, create a clean heart for me and renew
a steadfast spirit within me."*
—Psalm 51:10, csb

"Reformation is making the crooked ways straight!"
—HB

"*A voice cries: 'In the wilderness prepare the way of the Lord; make straight in the desert a highway for our God.'*"
—Isaiah 40:3

"If His throne is built upon righteousness and justice, so should our lives be!"

—HB

"Righteousness and justice are the foundation of Your throne."
—Psalm 89:14, NKJV

"Our God is a just God! He is looking for just sons and daughters who will carry His justice and righteousness!"

—HK

*"God decided in advance to adopt us into his own family
by bringing us to himself through Jesus Christ."*
—Ephesians 1:5, NLT

> *"Personal reformation means we partner with God in making the crooked ways straight in us! Then God partners with us, releasing His authority and power to bring reformation to others and our nation!"*
>
> —HK

"But thanks be to God, that you who were once slaves of sin have become obedient from the heart to the standard of teaching to which you were committed, and, having been set free from sin, have become slaves of righteousness."
—Romans 6:17–18

"But I will hope continually and will praise you more and more. My mouth will tell about your righteousness and your salvation all day long, though I cannot sum them up."
—Psalm 71:14–15, CSB

> "If we encounter His presence daily by going into His throne room, we should come out with a stronger desire for what His throne is built upon, righteousness and justice."
>
> —HB

> *"My heart has heard you say, 'Come and talk with me.'
> And my heart responds, 'LORD, I am coming.'"*
> —PSALM 27:8, NLT

> "Do not fear, for I am with you; do not be afraid, for I am your God. I will strengthen you; I will help you; I will hold on to you with my righteous right hand."
> —Isaiah 41:10, csb

> "The church, Christians—you and me—we are the answer to injustice! He has anointed us for this purpose!"
>
> —HB

"Be strong and courageous. Do not be afraid; do not be discouraged, for the Lord your God will be with you wherever you go."
—Joshua 1:9, NIV

*"You prepare a table before me in the presence of my enemies;
you anoint my head with oil; my cup overflows."*
—Psalm 23:5, CSB

"Christianity isn't about religion and laws—it is about relationship, or daily encounters, with the Lord."

—HB

> *"But just as He who called you is holy, so be holy in all you do, for it is written: 'Be holy, because I am holy.'"*
> —1 Peter 1:15–16, BSB

"But for me it is good to be near God; I have made the Lord GOD my refuge, that I may tell of all your works."
—PSALM 73:28, ESV

"Daily encounters is just spending time in His presence, in the Bible, in prayer, in talking to Him, and in worship every single day! These daily encounters will transform your life!"

—HB

"But I will sing of your strength and will joyfully proclaim your faithful love in the morning. For you have been a stronghold for me, a refuge in my day of trouble."
—Psalm 59:16, csb

"He put a new song in my mouth, a hymn of praise to our God. Many will see and fear, and they will trust in the Lord."
—Psalm 40:3, csb

"The LORD your God is in your midst, a mighty one who will save; he will rejoice over you with gladness; he will quiet you by his love; he will exult over you with loud singing."
—ZEPHANIAH 3:17

"You guide me with your counsel, leading me to a glorious destiny."
—Psalm 73:24, NLT

"Miracles happen in a moment, but healing takes place in a season."

—HB

"I am like a miraculous sign to many, and you are my strong refuge."
—Psalm 71:7, csb

"When we acknowledge that miracles happen, we must acknowledge the Author of them."

"He heals the brokenhearted and binds up their wounds."
—Psalm 147:3

> "Surely your goodness and love will follow me all the days of my life, and I will dwell in the house of the LORD forever."
> —PSALM 23:6, NIV

"God can and will heal it all if you offer it up to Him."

—HB

*"Put your hope in the Lord, because the Lord's love
never fails. He sets his people completely free."*
—Psalm 130:7, NIRV

"In all these things we are more than conquerors through him who loved us."
—Romans 8:37

"Call to me and I will answer you, and will tell you great and hidden things that you have not known."
—Jeremiah 33:3

> "But he said to me, 'My grace is sufficient for you, for my power is made perfect in weakness.' Therefore, I will boast all the more gladly about my weaknesses, so that Christ's power may rest on me."
> —2 Corinthians 12:9, NIV

"Weariness sounds and feels like comfort in giving up! Remember, the Holy Spirit is your comforter and helper—never give up!"

> *"Come to Me, all you who are weary and burdened, and I will give you rest."*
> —Matthew 11:28, BSB

"Deliverance is easy in His presence."

"My yoke is easy, and my burden is light."
—Matthew 11:30

"He will be the sure foundation for your times, a rich store of salvation and wisdom and knowledge; the fear of the Lord is the key to this treasure."
—Isaiah 33:6, niv

> *"When we fear only the Lord, we will do His will, no matter what the cost is."*
>
> —HB

> "And the Spirit of the Lord shall rest upon him, the Spirit of wisdom and understanding, the Spirit of counsel and might, the Spirit of knowledge and the fear of the Lord. And his delight shall be in the fear of the Lord."
> —Isaiah 11:2–3

> "But you will receive power when the Holy Spirit has come upon you, and you will be my witnesses in Jerusalem and in all Judea and Samaria, and to the end of the earth."
> —Acts 1:8

> *"God can and wants to use you. If you let Him, He will blow your mind!"*
>
> —

> "You did not choose me, but I chose you and appointed you so that you might go and bear fruit—fruit that will last—and so that whatever you ask in my name the Father will give you."
> —John 15:16, NIV

"Only our God can take our most shameful moments from our past and use them to set others free!"

> *"...the God who equipped me with strength
> and made my way blameless."*
> —Psalm 18:32

"For you equipped me with strength for the battle; you made those who rise against me sink under me."
—Psalm 18:39

"Exposing is never comfortable, but when you shine light on hidden things, the darkness that's been taunting you has to go."

—HB

> "The light shines in the darkness, and the darkness has not overcome it."
> —John 1:5

"He gives power to the faint, and to him who has no might he increases strength."
—Isaiah 40:29

"And let us not grow weary of doing good, for in due season we will reap, if we do not give up."
—Galatians 6:9

"You must draw a line in the sand that you will never give up! Everything is possible with God!"

—HB

"For nothing will be impossible with God."
—Luke 1:37

> "LORD, you are my portion and my cup of blessing; you hold my future."
> —PSALM 16:5, CSB

"The future is bright for those who fear the Lord!"

> *"Now to him who is able to do far more abundantly than all that we ask or think, according to the power at work within us, to him be glory in the church and in Christ Jesus throughout all generations, forever and ever."*
> —Ephesians 3:20

"Fulfilling dreams should be about fulfilling God's dreams within us! And if they're His dreams within us accomplished by His power and the gifts He placed within us, then He gets all the glory!"

—HB

> "Then he said to me, 'This is the word of the LORD to Zerubbabel: Not by might, nor by power, but by my Spirit, says the LORD of hosts.'"
> —ZECHARIAH 4:6

"Instead of your shame you will receive a double portion, and instead of disgrace you will rejoice in your inheritance. And so you will inherit a double portion in your land, and everlasting joy will be yours."
—Isaiah 61:7, NIV

> "Just as you used to offer the parts of your body in slavery to impurity and to escalating wickedness, so now offer them in slavery to righteousness leading to holiness."
> —Romans 6:19, BSB

> "Laughter is a weapon; laughter lifts heavy burdens,
> heals broken hearts, shatters intimidation, and
> sends it back into the enemy's camp!"
>
>

"The joy of the Lord is your strength."
—Nehemiah 8:10

*"She is clothed with strength and dignity, and
she laughs without fear of the future."*
—Proverbs 31:25, NLT

"We laugh without fear of our future—this is who we are called to be."
—HB

"You reveal the path of life to me; in your presence is abundant joy; at your right hand are eternal pleasures."
—Psalm 16:11, CSB

"When you laugh in the face of the enemy and place your fear in the Lord, Satan's arrows bounce off you and right back at him! Don't let your joy or laughter be stolen!"

—HB

> "Finally, be strong in the Lord and in the strength of his might. Put on the whole armor of God, that you may be able to stand against the schemes of the devil."
> —Ephesians 6:10–11

> "Behold, I have given you authority to tread on serpents and scorpions, and over all the power of the enemy, and nothing shall hurt you."
> —Luke 10:19

"Your worship to Jesus places the devil under your feet!"

> *"The God of peace will soon crush Satan under your feet. The grace of our Lord Jesus Christ be with you."*
> —Romans 16:20

> *"But thanks be to God, who gives us the victory through our Lord Jesus Christ."*
> —1 Corinthians 15:57

"Your worship will lead you from victory to victory!"
—HB

> "For everyone who has been born of God overcomes the world. And this is the victory that has overcome the world—our faith."
> —1 John 5:4

"Do not worry about what to say or how to say it. At that time you will be given what to say, for it will not be you speaking, but the Spirit of your Father speaking through you."
—Matthew 10:19–20, NIV

"Use your voice and share your testimony everywhere you go, giving glory to God for what He did in your life while releasing faith into everyone around you whom God will set free too!"

—HB

> *"'For I know the plans I have for you,' declares the Lord, 'plans to prosper you and not to harm you, plans to give you hope and a future.'"*
> —Jeremiah 29:11, NIV

"When you receive true healing, you can leave a true legacy."

—HB

> *"...that the next generation might know them, the children yet unborn, and arise and tell them to their children, so that they should set their hope in God and not forget the works of God."*
> —Psalm 78:6–7

"He has anointed us to preach the Good News, meaning you can't fear using your voice by sharing your testimony and how Jesus has saved you with others!"

—KS

> *"Therefore go and make disciples of all nations, baptizing them in the name of the Father, and of the Son, and of the Holy Spirit, and teaching them to obey all that I have commanded you. And surely I am with you always, even to the end of the age."*
> —Matthew 28:19–20, BSB

"To bring revival and reformation to our land means our fear is in nothing but the Lord!"

> "Every valley shall be lifted up, and every mountain and hill be made low; the uneven ground shall become level, and the rough places a plain. And the glory of the Lord shall be revealed, and all flesh shall see it together, for the mouth of the Lord has spoken."
> —Isaiah 40:4–5

> *"Be set free from your past, unscarred and unashamed to share your story!"*
>
> —HB

> *"For I am not ashamed of the gospel, for it is the power of God for salvation to everyone who believes, to the Jew first and also to the Greek."*
> —Romans 1:16

*"You are a vessel of revival and reformation—it
is in you. Now it is time to release it!"*

—HB

> "The Spirit of the Lord God is upon me, because the Lord has anointed me to bring good news to the poor; he has sent me to bind up the brokenhearted, to proclaim liberty to the captives, and the opening of the prison to those who are bound."
> —Isaiah 61:1

"Now is the time to share your freedom story!"

—HB

Dear Writer,

Congratulations! You have finished writing the first draft of your freedom story! I encourage you to bring it back to the Lord and tell Him, "This is Yours, Lord. I am Yours. This story is Yours because You're the Author and Redeemer of my life, my story." If you do that, this is just the beginning of the journey the Lord will take you on with Him. He will remind you of more and heal every area until every part of your life is in His light, no longer any part of your past or present being hidden, which equals a free future! Everything surrendered to Jesus means slavery to nothing (except calling it an honor to be His bond servant). His holy conviction will come closer and be louder, allowing you to break old patterns forever. I pray that the more you write, the more you share, the freer you are.

I personally experienced this. The more I would write and share, the more He would bring up and set me free from. I remember going from joy to tears, tears to joy over and over as the Lord healed me through writing and remembrance. I encourage you to take Communion right now, to again remind yourself of what He did for you! He died on the cross for you! And when He took the first Communion with His disciples, He said, "Do this in remembrance of me" (1 Cor. 11:24). This means you will make many mistakes from here on out, there will be other moments you will fall short and sin, but remember what He did for you—He died so you could have life, and have it abundantly (John 10:10)! And remember, it is by both His blood and the word of your testimony that you conquer the enemy (Rev. 12:10–11)! So get out that Communion right now and remember what He did for you; examine yourself (1 Cor. 11:28) and completely surrender your life story to Him!

I encourage you to consistently encounter the Lord through remembrance. When you go back and remember the things you once did, writing about them, sharing them, remember, He set you free! Remember, by His stripes you are healed (Isa. 53:5)! Remember, He died for you and was risen on the third day for you (Matt. 28:5–6)! Remember, that life *lives* in you, that power *lives* in you, that freedom *lives* in you!

www.ingramcontent.com/pod-product-compliance
Lightning Source LLC
Chambersburg PA
CBHW020654060526